Bren Simmers

HASTINGS-

SUNRISE

NIGHTWOOD EDITIONS

2015

Nightwood Editions
P.O. Box 1779
Gibsons, BC VON 1VO
Canada
www.nightwoodeditions.com

TYPOGRAPHY & COVER DESIGN: Carleton Wilson
COVER IMAGE: Bren Simmers

Nightwood Editions acknowledges financial support from the Government of Canada
through the Canada Book Fund and the Canada Council for the Arts, and from the
Province of British Columbia through the British Columbia Arts Council and the Book
Publisher's Tax Credit.

This book has been produced on 100% post-consumer recycled, ancient-forest-free paper,
processed chlorine-free and printed with vegetable-based dyes.

Printed and bound in Canada.

LIBRARY AND ARCHIVES CANADA CATALOGUING IN PUBLICATION

Simmers, Bren, 1976-, author
Hastings–Sunrise / Bren Simmers.

Poems.
Issued in print and electronic formats.
ISBN 978-0-88971-310-9 (pbk.).--ISBN 978-0-88971-049-8 (pdf).

1. Vancouver (B.C.)--Poetry. I. Title.

PS8637.I47H38 2015   C811'.6   C2015-901126-4
                                     C2015-901127-2

TABLE OF CONTENTS

▲
N

21 × 13 blocks
Not to scale

Petals strung like popcorn
March 21

Trees fill in their dance cards
April 7

Crows karaoke with the alarm
April 19

Scouting alleys for lilacs
May 7

Open windows
May 25

Landscape formed by bright awnings:
Hong Hong Bakery, Pies 2 for $7,
Keys Cut Here. On Mr. Donair's spit,
the earth rotates. Papal smoke emits
from Polonia Sausage, semis shunt
downtown, second-growth steel glints
in the distance. This two-storey strip,
fat quarter of blocks still a livable scale
in a city where cranes hoist the skyline
toward Shangri-La.

Learning new streets on foot,
how long to grow routes, wear paths
from green grocer to deli, dim sum to tailor.
Beyond address, habit, what makes
home? Surely not the sour waft
of rendered chicken, nor the caged budgies
we watch waiting for a #14. People
who perch at our perimeters define
our edges. At work, I record

when the tree swallows return, the first
salmonberry pickpocketed by temperature.
From a third-storey apartment, park
uniform shucked, I survey shipyards,
the North Shore. Find the rhythms
of street trees, swing sets, glimpse
a larger pattern—the phenology of
panhandlers, brunch crowds, for sale
signs, my life reflected in what
I choose to record.

238 N. Kamloops—
Tyvek-wrapped,
I covet you already,
your bay windows,
west-facing porch.
Weekly, I've tracked
your growth from concrete
footings to rising frame.
Modest shack, laneway
house big enough for
my love, our cat. A piano,
a garden, a window desk—
all that I imagine from behind
the rented metal fence.
Better yet, my love can
compose sonatas next door,
a laundry line to pulley notes
across. Frida had a bridge,
Georgia had Ghost Ranch.
Virginia, you understand,
I dream of four walls.

A spinning top from one spring to the next.
Equinox, Easter, the calendar advances
a row of red Xs, halts for circled
weddings, funerals, births.
Hopscotch between sticky notes:
laundry, cat litter, write vows.

Growing up, the chime of a grandfather clock
struck the hour. My father swore
it sped up as he got older.
Less time to do more. The pendulum's O
swings back and forth, a constant pulse.
Looking for a way out of my busy life,
what if I started looking for a way in?

Doesn't take much to reclaim a corner
from Slurpee cups and cigarette butts.
A shortcut transformed into a mini-park
with a bench, a few flowering shrubs,
a scraggly garden of cast-off
hostas, divided irises,
remnants welcome,

> even the parts of myself
> I cover up or reject.
> Quick to anger, despair.
> A friend's letter reminds,
> *It is your darkness that gives*
> *you your shine.*

Ten years on Vancouver Island.
I couldn't bear one more Garry oak cut
down for a Costco, one more mountainside
bulldozed into naked cul-de-sacs.
I returned to a city already ruined

and found people building
raised beds on boulevards,
growing roots, pushing back.

Penned on scrap cardboard:
Please don't steal the plants.

Dawn's metallic drum roll recalls
   that single bed we once shared.
Blinds left open to watch the sky

turn scarlet, colour of closed eyes.
   Waking to the roller-coaster flight
of woodpeckers. First kisses.

A pair of red-shafted flickers
   lapping ants with sticky tongues.
Four, five hours rest, before my love rose

to sketch songs on the loaned Wurlitzer.
   Now, we're often too tired,
blackout curtains block street lights

but not sirens and foghorns.
   When I lay my head on his chest,
prelude to sheet-stealing and sleep

positions a to z in our double bed,
   it's those woodpeckers I hear
inside his ribs, drumming.

Metal handle even with his shoulders, the boy
heaves forward. The goliath rears up
                    and chomps down,
ragged whitecaps of shorn and long grass
in its wake. The boy's father shouts
instructions over the din. I wish I had

someone to tell me never mow
barefoot. Eat your vegetables.
Take the long view in marriage,
this argument won't matter in ten years.

Watching the hand-off from father to son—
what will I pass on? Childless
by choice, who will I watch
from the window?
                    As his mother worries the glass
with a cloth, as the boy pushes
a swath into the future, bright yellow
            dandelions flare
under the whirling blade.

Judged on curb appeal, which exterior fits
ours? On after-dinner walks pretend
we own: pick your favourite house on this block,
the white-shuttered cottage or shoe-worn
Edwardian porch. Through architectural tropes
we test differences. But what of the interiors,
the back lanes where the real living happens?
Our routines don't align without effort.
I crave quiet into afternoons; my love plays
double bass in our one-bedroom. All
the negotiations over headphones, time alone.
He loves the cottage, its small footprint,
says we don't need much. True.
I still covet a fireplace, a hammock,
doors we can close. Night after night
these questions act as cardinal points
at the crossroads.

Local mascots, the wooden mannequins
in front of Laughing Bean Coffee
change their positions daily:
foxtrot, karate chop, strut Canucks
jerseys on game nights, high-five
commuters who slow to read placards:
his *Freshly Baked* and hers
I love his hot muffins.

Milk steaming at espresso machines,
the barista asks the next in line,
What'll it be today, Henry?
A simple question triggers
envy. To be known, a regular
drinking chai and playing Scrabble
with my love, to let down
my guard long enough
to be seen, called out
of anonymity.

Night of nesting dolls,
many layers held
inside this one:
cocktails on the balcony,
supper at eight, the after-
dinner doubles games,
while kids pump legs
on swing sets.
At sundown, an old man
shuffles three times
around the park. Nightly,
I've started to look for
his cross-country gait,
tan paperboy cap,
started to call him *ours*.
Then falls the deep blue
scrim and the few
stars we can spot
amid shipyard cranes
and lights on Grouse.
So brief,
the smallest doll
is sleep.

Map of Neighbourhood Swings

xx

x
o   o

o

o
xx

x

x

x   x

xx   xx

x tree swings
o swing sets

▲
N
19 × 10 blocks
Not to scale

When public space grows scarce,
    tennis courts get taken over
for badminton, bike polo, skateboarding.
Training ground for unicyclers, kick-boxers,
pyrotechnicians and my favourite:
seniors in matching white

sun hats. At dawn, they coax stiff bodies
through sequence, *part the wild horse's mane,
wave hands like clouds*, while I wait
for the kettle to boil. Small comfort
to know someone's awake before me,
    needle at sea bottom.

Insect clouds
June 5

Trio sonata for weed whacker, saw and nail gun
June 16

New, borrowed, blue
July 2

All the leisure a paycheque can afford
July 11

Bare arms, midnight
July 25

꒰♥

Dry pink sockets
where the eyes once
nestled. I flinch at first,
think the dog mad
then realize   and hold out
she can't see   an unsteady hand.
                      As I stroke the dog's
                      coarse fur, the owner
                      rounds the corner,
                      asks, *Do you know her?*

As if she belongs to the entire block,
not to him. The dog lopes ahead,
navigating by nose alone. When will I
belong to the city I was born in?
Accretion of salt water into skin,
a proportion of years.

Walking the same streets until
I know their every season.
Always one foot out, one foot in.
I forget the city belongs to everyone.
It's ours to claim.

The building next door has bedbugs
   again. A trio of mattresses by the dumpster.
Wide berth as we walk past. Touch wood—
   though once they're in, wood won't stop them.
Touch steel then. On the Bedbug Registry,
   a cluster of red dots surrounds our apartment
like front lines or angry bears. Hundreds
   exterminated this year for being hungry,
dumpster diving near suburban homes built for
   Goldilocks. We, who crave a yard, itch.

꙳

Strollers stake out shady maples
    while kids ride noodles
        in the wading pool,
bob in water wings.

Moms up to their
    knees cool off, while
        tweens sight targets
with Super Soakers.

Shrieks, splashes, running in
    and out in T-shirts, shorts.
        Nothing like free water
in summer. The beach

too far to walk. This park a shared
    backyard, erases divides, draws
        zebra foals and lion pups
to the watering hole.

Friday night at Hastings Park.
Our beer in plastic cups. Pre-race,
the announcer tells us to look for
    a big ass, a line of muscle along the abs
    as horses bounce and prance past
patio tables, retirees with circled stats,
hipsters in fedoras, weekend warriors,
families and first-timers craving novelty.

The regulars drink inside,
beer rings stamped on betting slips.
Bred for impulse, live-feed TVs.
Minutes till the starting gun,
exam hush as their pencils wager
cubicle earnings against Luck
of the Devil. A flurry of hunches
before *crack*.

Cramped on their saddles,
jockeys jack-in-the-box.
Horses try to outrun
whips. Call it sport or
9 to 5 odds I can't watch.
Close my eyes.
A wall of noise
at the finish line.

Blame MASH
for my addiction to MLS.
Not the TV show, but the '80s
fortune-telling game starring you
and your latest crush Chris/Jeff/Steve,
seven babies and a red Mustang.
Recess spent giggling with friends,
knowing a mansion was out of reach,
a shack unlikely, but certain
I'd own a house.
        Fast forward twenty-five years:
Chris is married with two kids,
Jeff's a gay journalist and Steve
manages a Safeway. Five percent down
has spawned sprawl, smog
and bank foreclosures.
I ask my ten-year-old self
what's wrong with renting
an apartment? People in New York
or LA can't afford to own unless
they're cardiologists or movie stars.
Many flatshare into their forties.
This tenement marks us
as ordinary cosmopolitans.

❧

Light as a paper clip, steel
    and box elder that twists
round my finger, a reminder

of this new life. Where it rubs
    a callus forms.
Slip it off to recall

who I was before. Worry
    I'll lose it
down gutter or drain. Slip it on,

invisible again. To hold space
    for self, insist on
sweetheart, love. Cleft-grafted

onto another to bear fruit,
    a scion braced
against future storms.

Or am I simply added onto,
    cambium growing
another ring of wood.

Winged insects lumber past—
        moths perhaps, drawn to the balcony's
light—as the horizon stretches its orange
canvas overhead and I enjoy the few
hours of the day I call mine

stacked in this hive. A closer look
reveals tiny wings beating double
        time to lift their pollen basket
three floors up, bodies dusted
with a day's labour, returning
to regurgitate nectar for the queen.

These stiffs clock more hours than me,
secrete then chew wax into
honeycomb, fill then cap,
forage till dusk, and still
        they dance. I want to
ascribe pleasure to their waggle,
to their figure eights. Love
the work that pays the bills.
Take one last sip before
turning in.

Time Log: A Workbook[1]

168	hours in a week[2]
– ____	sleep
– ____	day job/commute/thought hours consumed
– ____	eating vegetables, not just eggs on toast
– ____	Yahoo/Google/Crackbook/YouBoob
– ____	procrastination/dawdling
= ____	left for forest bathing/books
	pie crust/potlucks/peeps
	chasing the cat/changing
	sheets/sex/me[3]

---

1 On the back of an envelope, track where one week gets spent and why there feels like less time to stay connected, despite tweets, texts, chats, all the apps.

2 College kids bike play polo all day in the tennis courts. Envious of their free time, I forget we're all given the same twenty-four.

3 Balance, a pendulum swinging back and forth. Write at the expense of exercise. Read or get enough sleep. Ask yourself, *What is the next necessary thing?* Then do that.

Height of summer.

Not the early days of gorging, but the plateau.

Days ironed flat as a sheet.

Residents stoop-sit.

Bathing suits drip.

Back of the knees sweat.

On a late-night walk, heat opens

barred windows and doors:

❧

Map of Open Doors

( )   ( ) ( )   ( )   (a) ( )

                              ( )

                              ( )
                              (a) ( )   ( )
              (a) ( )   (a)

       (a)

                                   ( )

                                   ( )
       (a)

       ( )   ( )

       ( ) ( )

At the corner of Lakewood & Charles,
someone's built a miniature
house with a glass door, its three
shelves filled with free books.
A crow drawn to tinfoil,
I stop to look, yank shiny
spines like new garden shoots
that birds beak for grubs:
a how-to foot massage,
a pop-up history of the bra,
a farm-life memoir.
Drop one off, or scrawl a message
in chalk, *Block party this Friday,*
or like deer, browse on
deckle edges, dog-eared pages.
The book box a community
hub cycling our ideas through
living rooms, fortifying roots
as nutrients do in soil.

Air quality advisory
Aug 6

Wasps circle for scraps
Aug 18

Back-to-school ads push iPads
Sept 4

Sidewalk bowling with horse chestnuts
Sept 21

Squirrels, we scatter-hoard our affections
Oct 13

Too tired to live the postcard—
     bike the Seawall, swim at Third Beach,
     sample 213 flavours at La Casa Gelato
     from parmesan to popcorn, wasabi to hot dog,
we read *New Yorker* cartoons in bed. Caption contest
to cover, our humour aligns, diverges, as we scan
the "Goings On" for one more laugh.

In the city that never sleeps, do people
exploit the nightlife or do they stay home in slippers
like us, read Pitchfork, watch YouTube in Brooklyn
where they sell *I can't afford to* ❤ NY T-shirts.
Is proximity enough? Small fry,

big pond. Runoff filtered through organs.
Too tired to consume the just-announced,
five stars, openings, so why be here at all?
On weekends, seek refuge, holdfast

our hood, its walkability score of 87.
All our errands in four blocks. Coffee
shops, cheap sushi—the city sells choice
on every corner. If pressed, we'll say
we stay for the option to say yes.

People we pass every day
become our landscape,
and we, theirs.
A friend tells time
by where she passes
the same woman
on her way to work,
which block. On
Granville, it's opera man,
who belts out Puccini,
Rossini, Verdi maybe,
as he strolls the sidewalk.
Here, it's the woman
in a tiara begging
outside McDonald's,
the old man we watch for
at sundown, and he for us.

૪〜

Businesses, opened:

Campagnola Roma
Mac-Talla Cycles
The Red Wagon Café
East Village Bakery
Bridal Boutique
Nutters Natural Foods
Flowers N More

Businesses, closed:

Toby's Teriyaki Bowl
Seri Malaysia Restaurant
Sunrise Gifts Fashion
Lisbon Bakery
Rogers Video
Mr. Donair
J.J. Motor Cars[4]

---

4 Dairy Queen and Church's Chicken give way to gluten-free cookies on square white plates. Lineups of copycat plaid, ten speeds and dark-rimmed glasses outside the diner serving pulled pork pancakes; khakis and pumps under heat lamps at the wine bar nibble local octopus salad. A virus duplicating itself all over the city. Urban pioneers with arts degrees settle first—*Dear god that's us*—displace the original tenants. Then come the hipsters, the DINKs. When young families and yuppies buy in, it's time to find a new host cell.

The Pacific National Exhibition brings rain and blue ribbons,
Icarus pigeons, cows with keg-size udders, Super Mario
Brothers sculpted from canned goods, PG-rated sand
mermaids, equestrian sports, chainsaw demos, roller
coasters, bumper cars, 70 km/h rides, g-force post-
gorge on candy corn, chili dogs, mini-donuts,
no wonder washroom lineups belch along.
Pig races on the hour where kids in pink
smocks with rubber nipples attached
call *Suey!* and garner laughs before
Britney Spare Ribs bests Kevin
Bacon in a thirty-second dash.
The end of summer viewed
from bleachers in the beer
garden, aging '80s rock
stars rehash their one
hit, while past-your-
bedtimes stream
out wanting
one more
kick.

Vacuflo, bay windows,
wall-to-wall carpet, my childhood
spent stocking-toed in show homes
with napkin-sketches of where
our furniture would go.
        Dreams built on Visa,
line of credit. What I know
of being an adult. Trying on
the rooftop deck, the Master Chef BBQ
on Pender Street, pretending
the shoe fits—
                it's not that
my love doesn't crave a hearth,
he appreciates a tree-lined street
without wanting to own it.
Neither of us willing to sacrifice
more working hours.
I don't know if this house
habit is more wound
than pleasure. Canker
the tongue worries in the mouth;
teeth bite down on it
again and again.

Driving home in the slow stop crawl
of a Tuesday commute, what I have
bumper to bumper against what I want.
A polyester uniform affords a life,
but not a front stoop, a garden.
Full-time feels like a clear-cut;
family and friends a scenic fringe.
Is there an accident on the bridge?
Why is it so backed up? The sky black
with crows exiting eastbound
each evening to roost.

A hundred cars to the off-ramp. Stuck,
a feedback loop of buy more, work more.
Spot the odd crow in counterflow
darting in and out of the surge.
A single sine wave. Eyes measure
the distance between peaks:
yoga class, Friday-night Shiraz,
the freefall in between. To be that crow.
Grow feathers, hollow bones,
scavenge a different wealth
from notes, berries, books.

First rain in weeks, waking to
    wind, wet streets. Applause of car wheels
on slick asphalt. Showers, not yet heavy,

baritone. Leonard Cohen on the stereo next door.
    Permission to stay in, nimbostratus
pulled up to my chin. Take a cue from the weather

and reflect heat back. Working on the tracks, my father
    learned to quench thirst by placing a stone
under his tongue. Soon, it became part of his mouth.

What of a word? *Married* a month now,
    husband still falters in my throat. Needing to cycle
through a year of runoff, evaporation,

before we become familiar as cirrus, cumulus.
    The water that falls outside my window as
old as the earth.

Each fall, I forget red was there all along,
    yellow, orange only show
in the leaf after the work's done.
Hues helped by sunlight, frost.
Cambridge Street a jackpot.

Leaves staged in neat piles for toddlers
to jump on. An unofficial block party.
Families kick crimson drifts, watch a leaf
whirl from branch to ground. Spin a petiole,
thread through buttonhole.

Cue the leaf-blower. Enter the decibel
of hearing loss, as some schmo blasts
his yard, then sidewalk, of spectacle.
He's robbing us of ritual—to watch leaves dry
or crunch into lace underfoot.

Limbic matchsticks flare,
    then gust by gust blow out.
Alone in his Sunday chores, he's still
part of the crowd drawn outdoors
to mark this red hour.

Map of Autumn Tree Colour[5]

```
        r    r    r    r    r

                  o    o    y

                  y    b

                  r    r    r

                  y    b

        o    r    r

        o    r    o

   o    y    y    y

   o    y         r

        r         r
```

▲
N

10 × 6 blocks

Not to scale

5 Just as scientists in the Hoh Rainforest protect one square inch of silence, neighbourhoods have epicentres of quiet also, where the noise of main streets doesn't reach, where wind in the leafy canopy dominates. Stillness extends outward from Cambridge and Eton Streets where I walk the same route through all seasons. Watch buds appear, flowers bloom, leaves fall. Meditate my own changes. Identities clung to and let go. Allegiance shifts—family to friends to love—though inside there remains a silence that will always be my own.

Trending this week:
zombie princesses, ghost cupcakes,
DIY graves—rake leaves into a mound,
add Styrofoam headstone. *Not too big,*
not too small, the pillowcase still reigns
as loot bag of choice. At five o'clock,
the first Transformers and Dora
the Explorers totter out.
An off-key chorus of *trick or treat.*
Next year, vow to carve pumpkins
for the balcony, throw Tootsie Rolls
three storeys down. Fewer houses
with lights on—the skeleton crew
of pirates, vampires and Angry Birds
have farther to run. Safer at Hogwarts,
at the mall? From strangers who
ring our doorbell: telemarketers,
Jehovahs, Girl Guides and high
schoolers selling raffle tickets,
something good to eat. The only time
of year we open our doors
willing to give.

The construction stalled
at 238 N. Kamloops
or gone interior, and I feel
shut out of my own daydream,
the city where I was born.
My parents' first house cost
$28,000. On Hastings
they're pre-selling one-bedrooms
starting in the low 300s. Opportunity
cost for a mountain backdrop.
Can we make a home without a house,
borrow a shell like hermit crabs
to protect the softness
claws can't defend?
We joke about moving
to a fictional small town
named Saska–Wollup.
Consider buying a foreclosure
in the Midwest, where we could
own another's loss outright.
Find a rent increase notice
taped to our door. Stare
at the mountains in response.
Zero babies, a Toyota—MASH failed
to predict topographical mansions.
Like spawning salmon returning
to coastal streams, these peaks
imprinted in blood, my true north.
Without them, a weather vane
whipping circles in a storm?

Wind warning in effect.
Slamming cupboards, silence.
After a decade of living alone,
I'm learning to coexist. To rinse dishes,
not drop tea bags in the sink. Lock myself
in the bathroom, my mother's trick. Avoid
mood transference. 50–70 km/h gusts, hard pelt
of leaves. Pinned to the chain-link fence
       like classroom art, red scrawls
       suspended until the storm relents.
I'm sorry, blame PMS, Mercury in retrograde,
and they slump into sheaves
for the street cleaner
to collect.

Lake chains form in the tennis courts
Nov 6

Days bookended by dark
Nov 22

Mailbox stuffed with gift ideas
Dec 10

Shortbread torpor
Dec 27

Our old man's shuffle now a march.
His park circuit doubled; we spot him
morning and night. As he clocks past
our balcony, he glances up.
I want to wave, but worry he won't
wave back, or that we'll enter into
an unspoken contract.

Retired, my father also circles the park
in a nearby suburb, chats with neighbours
about houses, assesses roofs, their risk
of flooding. In unexpected ways
our jobs leak out of us; an insurance
adjuster, all those billable losses
absorbed into tears, into blood.

Do they know his name, call him
old man? Look for his navy coat,
brisk walk, out there in sleet and sun,
a semi-synchronous orbit
that registers in their *umwelt*.

On days he doesn't show—fear
heart attack, old-age home. Our lives
buoyed by others' routines. Water drops
that ripple outwards, an *umgebung*
of overlapping concentric rings.

Development Application No DE413659
Formerly known as 2539–2599 East Hastings Street[6]

---

6 Demolition day reveals a four-digit
phone number painted on brick from a time
formerly known as Hastings Townsite.
A small plaque at New Brighton Park shouts
in small caps HERE VANCOUVER BEGAN. A post office,
hotel, ferry, dock and road formerly known as
Khanamoot and towering cedars before that.
My memories only span a generation back.
Rotary phones and tape cassettes, Expo '86.
Gone—the working class boarding house
where my dad grew up. *If you didn't have
the seven-cent fare for the streetcar downtown
you just hopped on or walked.* All that's left
are street names, stories layered like insurance
decals on rusted Dodge vans. Our lives
formerly known as.

About small towns, we joke
no more. We can buy a house
outright in rural Saskatchewan
for $30,000, a fixer-upper
in a town big enough to have groceries,
a library, bar, bank—though not just
any sour gas town will do.
Pastoral dreams of porch swings
hijacked by an oil boom. Co-ops
drowned by pumpjacks, corporations
own the rights below the soil.
     Say we find our Saska–Wollup,
what of the trade-offs, topography.
Red vs. blue states. The non-
negotiables. How close to
the nearest airport, farmer's market,
music festival, yoga class? We talk
the bottle empty over dinner.
We could import our people,
start a community of artists.
Ha! I must be drunk.
Draw on the back of a ticket stub:

Vancouver   Saska–Wollup

Charcuteries, gluten-free
bakeries

Polite anonymity

Thriller flash mobs,
yarn bombs

Hipster toques

Retrospectives,
world premieres

Something missing

Pickled carrots,
Saskatoon berries

No ID required for parcel
pickup

Porch quiet: crickets, owls

Friends who vote differently

Lamb bakes, rodeos,
tractor trade shows

For three days, artists open their doors,
studios marked by a black metal crow.
Print a map, plot a route or just pinball, follow
the crowds at the Eastside Culture Crawl.
Dizzy with art, we tweet over travel mugs.
Did you see the ceramic hand grenades? The price tag
on that coffee table? #feltednests. More
than the canvas hung on the walls,
it's the bathtub in the corner
we covet, the view of the shipyard,
paintbrushes, toothbrush and fork
in the same jar by the sink. Put your big rocks
in first, my brother once told me—
smaller pebbles will fit around them.
A friend shares a studio with eight others
and a wood saw. Bring earplugs,
a room divider and *git 'er done.*
Put aside excuses, income-to-rent
calculations, and start
living the life you want.

Carnival of sheer wattage, six blocks
of blow-up Santas and snow globes.
Some wire every bulb they've got,
the Technicolor smarts like a sunburn
while others prefer Martha motifs, icicles,
grazing reindeer, silver wreaths.

Spectacle sprung after a B & E turned
murder. Residents fought to reclaim
Trinity Street with bright memorial.
A decade later, a local attraction.
Families on foot vote for best block,
best house. *The one with the train
or the life-size sleigh?*

Excessive, perhaps, a waste
of electricity, but who can't use a little
nudge through a dark time? Even a token
string will do. A fire hazard—
trees aren't allowed in our apartment,
so we deck the chandelier with '40s glass
ornaments from my mother,
our housewarming.

Months she spent cross-stitching
a stocking for a son-in-law.
Each *X* a wish, a letting go.
Lost on me—until I see two stockings
thumbtacked into the kitchen wall.

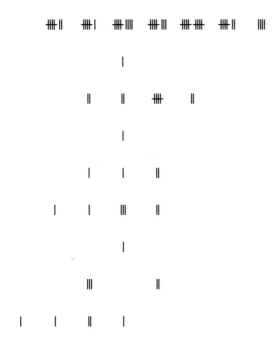

Map of Christmas Lights [7]

⟨N⟩

9 × 8 blocks

Not to scale

---

7 *Three on the left, two on the right—did you get that?* On a folded square map, make a tally mark for each lighted house. *Do trees in windows count?* When I stop to scribble notes or point, my love reminds me to be discreet—we may be posing as urban geographers, but to some we'll appear thieves. Block by block, we plot a transect north down Kamloops, all the way to Trinity Street, speculate a hypothesis between the number of lighted houses and folks who say hello to each other.

Parking lot full by 10 a.m., we join the dozen fleeces at the trail-head. Buckle up snowshoes. Smug to have gotten out early, rat race won before we've begun. *The Seymour Grind*, I joke. Metal teeth sink into slick narrow path, more bobsled than snow pack. We run down steep hills, try not to face plant. Feign athleticism. Step aside so people can pass, some say *Thanks*, others scowl, forgetting they're part of the crowd.

Cresting Dog Mountain, we clamber for a choice spot. Below us, the city ghosts a Pac-Man grid. Look for landmarks: Lions Gate Bridge, shipyard cranes, New Brighton Park. *Can you see our block?* The 360° view gives context to housing costs. Snap a few pictures for a status update. Faceboast why we live here. Call it content. Way down, come to a thin bridge of snow between us and the meltwater below. Test pixels with a pole, uncertain how long this filter will hold.

Plates cleared, coffee poured, siblings orbiting
between rooms, catch-up conversations
over scattered toys. Months since we last met,
and we all live in the same town. Something's wrong
with our grandfather clock—it's losing time.
Yesterday we were a pack of pillowcase clowns.
Today, grey in our hair and our parents old.
At sixty-five, my dad's outlived both his father and brother.
What is home, if not family, blood and chosen.
Without that mirror, blind? My dad knows
this city grows claustrophobic, tells me, *Go,
find your cabin in the woods.* Niece and nephew
play fire station. Sound the alarm. Their faces grow
older on the fridge. I grow into a stranger.
More coffee anyone? Three generations
briefly, once more.

Counting snowdrops
Jan 14

Binge-watching Netflix
Feb 3

Light until six o'clock
Feb 22

Green pinpricks
March 10

January circles its red pen, all finances, fitness,
then draws a different kind of wish list:
more sleep, less stress, feel like an athlete.
Each year, my friend chooses an intention.
Her old word was *thrive*, her new one
love. What's yours?
                        I'm caught;
haven't been doing the work
of sitting with uncertainty, quick to reach
for a glass of wine, a movie, buy a book when
I haven't read the stacks I own. *Abundance*—
I blurt, then amend to *sufficiency*.
Happiest when living out of a suitcase:
a pair of clean socks, two shirts.

Last winter, we subsisted on

69-cent oranges and spray-painted

tags. Downtown Eastside caught

a cursive virus of *I love you.*

Call it street art or resistance,

my outlook altered by a glance:

on the Pandora Park fence,

unseen hands have woven

bright strips of fabric

to read ♥ > $

꿔

5:30 a.m., still dark—
a woman in a fetal crouch sobs
on the sidewalk, her voice cracking
like ice against a ship's hull.
No one leans out, yells, *Shut up.*
Scared to ask, it could be catching.
Windows close, earplugs found,
while she, tragic chorus, calls.
Actors and audience both,
what in a city do we owe
each other? No script exists for
the security guard who performs
magic tricks, the man in slippers
who scowls at us but sings,
Here chicky chicky to his hens.
For the couple who found
my wallet lost on East Hastings
and returned it intact,
who simply said,
We're neighbours.

On the corner of Hastings and Slocan
we fight over official words,
May 23 (A) 233 (B) 287
za, *taj*, troll the dictionary for *qi*
and other cheap moves, *You stole my triple word*,
July 18 (A) 256 (B) 214
trounce each other, laud highest scores,
create rituals that bind. We jib, we cuss,
Sept 4 (A) 290 (B) 257
we *adze* grievances out.
Our notebook archives early games
Oct 27 (A) 319 (B) 299
at campgrounds, cross-border visits,
Bellingham, East Van, the Laughing Bean—
Dec 15 (A) 251 (B) 241
now part of our recorded historicity,
all the sedimentary layers
Feb 11 (A) 247 (B) 299
that under pressure form rock.

Overnight, street banners switch
from Hastings–Sunrise to East Village.

We've been rebranded by business
and their bid to attract more
young families now that the graffiti's down.

Gone is the reference to East Hastings
that kept nervous buyers away.
An overlooked gem, a pedestrian hub,
sold signs pox the block. Homeowners rejoice;
tenants dig trenches.

What drew us here: cheap rent,
    hole-in-the-wall diners, mixed incomes,
    a community with a pulse
soon wallpapered by boutiques.

Fight or flight.

Neighbourhood plans and letters only stall
the process. SUVs will tailgate us
to the next town. Density inevitable,
a stand of alders knocked down
for Rivendale townhomes.

The third option, hard work:
to dig in, grow roots, act like we plan
to live here forever, even if
we may not stay for good.

Chickadees chitter through treetops,
masked bank robbers.
    Juncos in hot pursuit,
their black and white tail feathers
flash like sirens.

The birds return with their questions,
call *cheeseburger* from fence posts,
    stake territory under eaves,
beak twigs into branches,
don't await our answers.

They gather moss, dog hair,
and dryer lint to line the nest,
then lift their tails for a quick
cloacal kiss.

In the coniferous dark, I nestle
into your arm crook
smell of cedar and hemlock, salt.
Mon mari. We're family now.
Choose this.

When Carmen, the cashier with the longest lines—
seven thousand customer names memorized—
asks me mine, I feel like Norm Peterson
at the green grocer. When I worked till,
my regulars had IOU cards, names penned
on top. No memory tricks required.
If Google Earth can be trusted, my old corner
store is now called Tomley's Market.
Twenty years ago, all I felt was my skin.
Hip-check the checkout wheel
into spin. Pores, freckles, scars since.
Paths worn into side streets. In twenty years,
Donald's will wear a six-storey condo.
New owners won't know before,
their clock starts now. As Carmen bags
my groceries, we volley the weather,
that inexhaustible genre—all the time
I'm thinking, she knows my name.
Is it enough to belong
to a particular time and place?

Plum or cherry, which comes first
      and how to tell them apart
when concrete traps heat, and trees

in the city centre break records.
      Kyoto data tracks
earlier blooms, a spike in temperature.

Twitter feed of melting sea ice,
      colony collapse
while we picnic under pink ribbons,

kiss again like we mean it.
      Bodies brief as blossoms.
Drawn to plum's sweet scent,

sakura's notched petals, horizontal
      lines on bark.
Late dark and early light growth—

tree rings form as we kiss
      under canopies,
as confetti drifts fill the gutters.

On foot to the book box, I find
Live now etched in wet cement.
The world full of counter-crow, I only need
to look: yarn-bombed trees, boulevard graffiti
that reads *Remember to breathe.*

To think of what was, an exercise in longing.
That city, that self, no longer exists.
The landmarks in our mental maps shift.
All we have: what the city can be.
This week the girl learning to unicycle

in the tennis courts let go
of the fence and found balance,
sign letters from a marquee adorn
the brow of a house, spell out *Be okay.*
On a low branch, someone's tied

a plastic bird. Each morning, look to see
it's still there. I'll stay as long as
it takes to finally say yes. Jump
both feet in. When two boys jostle
the bird to the ground, I call out,

insist they put it back. How quickly
I've grown attached. These streets
my own almanac, changes tracked,
as one by one, flight feathers
moult, turn black.

Map of Neighbourhood Routes

```
                              p p p p p p p p p p p
                              p                        NB
                              p l l l l l l l l
                              p L l l l l l l
                              p l
                         P l l l l l l l
              e b e b e b X e e e e e e e e e e e LB
                 e b          e D e e e e e e e e e e
                 e b                  MP
                 e b                  b
                 e b                  b
                 e b                  b
                 e b                  b
    e e e e e e e e e e e b            b
    e                     b            b
    e e e e e e e e e e e e B b b b b b b b b b b b b
```

b	book box route	L	laneway house
e	errand route	LB	laughing bean
l	laneway house route	MP	mini-park
p	park route	NB	new brighton park
B	book box	P	pandora park
D	donald's market	X	home

▲
N

21 × 13 blocks

Not to scale

Flickers drill telephone poles
March 21

Ankles exposed
April 7

Lawnmowers song-in-the-round
April 19

Chestnut blossom ice cream cones
May 7

Sidewalk chalk, hopscotch
May 25

ACKNOWLEDGEMENTS

I wish to thank the Canada Council for the Arts, the Banff Centre for the Arts and the Vermont Studio Center for financial assistance and offering me space and time to work on this project.

Thanks also to the editors of *Event Magazine*, *The Fiddlehead* and *Arc Poetry Magazine*, who published earlier versions of these poems, and to Silas White and Nightwood Editions for believing in this book.

I am truly indebted to Barbara Klar, who encouraged me to dig deeper and to put myself in these poems. A big thank you goes to Jill Boettger, Chelsea Bolan, Ariel Gordon, Maleea Acker and Elena Johnson who read and commented on earlier versions of this manuscript.

I also wish to thank: Vivienne McMaster for the author photo; Regan Taylor, best neighbour ever, who let me write in her apartment while she was at work; and Peter Lawrance for introducing me to phenology and the idea of micro-seasons.

A shout out to Hastings–Sunrise for insisting I pay attention to my life in the present moment, and to our old man, whose name I never learned. His daily presence changed the way I thought about urban neighbourhoods and belonging.

Thanks to all my peeps for conversations about finding "home" in Vancouver and elsewhere. Much love to Adam Hill, urban geographer, revision coach and *mon mari*.

This book is for my family: blood and chosen.

ABOUT THE AUTHOR

Bren Simmers is the author of one previous book of poetry, *Night Gears* (Wolsak and Wynn, 2010). She is the winner of an *Arc Poetry Magazine* Poem of the Year Award, was a finalist for *The Malahat Review*'s Long Poem Prize and has been twice longlisted for the CBC Poetry Prize. Her work has been anthologized in *Alive at the Center: Contemporary Poems from the Pacific Northwest* (Ooligan, 2013). She currently lives in Squamish, BC.